Original title:
Leaves and Light

Copyright © 2025 Creative Arts Management OÜ
All rights reserved.

Author: Evelyn Hartman
ISBN HARDBACK: 978-1-80581-853-3
ISBN PAPERBACK: 978-1-80581-380-4
ISBN EBOOK: 978-1-80581-853-3

## The Subtle Artistry of Change

Beneath the trees, the whispers play,
Colors shift in a bright ballet.
One day it's green, then gold the next,
Nature's pranks leave us perplexed.

The winds have secrets, a chuckle or two,
Tickling branches, a leafy review.
Rustling stories from every edge,
More twisty than a stitchy hedge!

A squirrel dashes, acorn in tow,
His cargo, a treasure, just stealing the show.
But watch out for rain; it's a slip and a slide,
Nature's slapstick, let's all take a ride!

In this wild dance, we all take part,
Giggling with joy, it's a leafy art.
Twisting and turning with smiles so bright,
In this theater of nature, what pure delight!

## Refractions of Time in Nature's Palette

A riddle unfolds in the morning's tease,
As shadows shuffle with the gentle breeze.
One moment's a globe, the next is a square,
Geometry's game in the open air.

The sun takes a stroll, a mischievous spark,
Playing hide and seek till it makes its mark.
Dappled patterns dance on the ground,
Like nature's jester, it skips around.

Birch trees gossip with the gnarled old oak,
Sharing their tales with each jovial poke.
A playful breeze carries laughter anew,
As shadows pirouette in viridian hue.

Moments stretch long, or zip by in a blink,
Nature's own clock, who's got time to think?
When ordinary sounds become pure delight,
We bask in the chaos, from day until night.

## Shimmering Petals and Silhouettes

There's a dance with the breeze,
A waltz of funny forms,
They twirl in the sun's tease,
Playing dress-up in warm swarms.

Silly shadows creep and roam,
Chasing giggles down the lane,
They sneak back to their leafy home,
Wearing outfits of sunshine's stain.

## The Glow of Nature's Changing Seasons

As colors change, the trees turn bold,
They swap their hats with a wink,
Beneath them, critters, brave and old,
Craft plans for seasonal-fun, I think.

With scarves of gold and shoes so bright,
They prance around, a merry sight,
Hiding nuts for a feast at night,
While giving squirrels quite a fright!

## **Vivid Murmurs in the Twilight Canopy**

Whispers of humor drift in air,
As nighttime wears her sparkly gown,
The giggles rise from everywhere,
In the depths of the twilight town.

Owls hoot jokes of riddles and puns,
While crickets play their nightly tunes,
Bats swoosh by chasing all the fun,
In the glow of silly afternoon's moons.

## Sun-Kissed Sketches on Earthen Floors

Watch as shadows sketch delight,
On ground where tiny feet stomp,
A canvas played in morning's light,
Where silly sprites and critters romp.

With crayons made of dappled hues,
They scribble giggles on the way,
Creating paths where laughter brews,
As nature leaps to join their play!

## **Whispers of Sunlit Canopies**

In a bustling green world, they chatter and sway,
Their tickles make squirrels just giggle away.
A breeze plays a tune, with rustles it sings,
While birds drop their snacks, oh, what joy this brings!

Sunshine joins the party, in shadows they prance,
A dance of pure chaos, a woodland romance.
The critters all chuckle, in awe of the scene,
As branches play tag, oh, it's silly and keen!

## **Dappled Shadows on the Ground**

A patchwork of patterns, in fun they parade,
Smiles from the dappled, beneath stars that fade.
Bouncing around, with giggles they play,
As cheeky little critters get carried away!

The sun beams a wink, as shadows collide,
A hide-and-seek game, where giggles provide.
The ground hosts a festival, oh, what a scene,
With tickled pink faces, a joyful routine!

## **Golden Hues in Autumn's Embrace**


In colors of laughter, the world turns to gold,
Each brushstroke a jest, and the boldness unfolds.
They spin and they tumble, like ages of cheer,
While autumn confetti drops from up here!

Chasing the breeze, a swirling brigade,
Waving a hello, a chuckling parade.
With giggles that echo, as they twist and shout,
The bright hues of joy, what's this all about?

## Celestial Glimmers in the Grove

Stars peek through branches, a wink from above,
While critters gather 'round, in a cozy love!
The twinkle of fireflies, like giggles at night,
A comedy act, what a whimsical sight!

In shadows they tumble, creating a fuss,
With squeaks and with laughter, it's all quite a plus.
Oh, look at them jostling, a fumble, a fall,
Under the canopy, they're having a ball!

## **Tapestry Woven with Nature's Brush**

In the park where shadows play,
A squirrel steals snacks without delay.
The branches dance in a silly sway,
While giggling blooms get carried away.

With colors bright and hues askew,
A robin sings of a world brand new.
The grass has jokes, as it tickles your shoe,
While butterflies flutter, in a merry queue.

The sun drops hints like a prankster's cheer,
Soft whispers heard from all around here.
A mischievous breeze sneaks up near,
And swirls up giggles like a traditional beer.

Nature's canvas, both wild and free,
Artful antics in the bush and tree.
So tip your hats, and join the spree,
In this tapestry, come dance with glee.

## Flickers Among the Trees

A flicker here and a flicker there,
The critters play, with naught a care.
A wiggly worm, a dance so rare,
While shadows tango in the fresh air.

The bunnies mock with a hops and skip,
A jolly parade, on a joy-filled trip.
Each rustle whispers like a secret quip,
As nature chuckles, a comic script.

The shimmer glances at what it can catch,
An acorn rolls with a playful patch.
As critters gather for a little match,
Where laughter's the goal, more than a snatch.

Oh, the fun beneath the canopy high,
With twinkling winks from the broad blue sky.
So come, oh come, don't be shy,
Join the fables that flutter and fly!

## The Art of Decay and Radiance


Once upon a time, a tree turned round,
With branches fracturing under their sound.
A dandy old leaf claimed its renown,
Waging a war with the ground so brown.

The earth's delight, a splatter of mud,
Told tales of laughter beneath a thud.
A wise old beetle, in truth a dud,
Claimed he could swim in a puddle of blood.

Yet as the colors shimmied down,
A jester's cap sprouted from the crown.
Nature biked in the silliest town,
Where chuckling roots threw a frown upside down.

Artful decay, a laugh in disguise,
With autumn's wink and mischief in the skies.
So gather your joy, and let's be wise,
In this merry mess, let laughter arise!

## Embered Pathways Through Nature

The paths we tread, a tapestry bold,
With crackling laughter that never grows old.
A wandering beetle, with stories untold,
Might add to the warmth as the day turns gold.

The winding trails dance with sparks of glee,
Where shadows play tricks, as wild as can be.
Each beetle's banter is wild, you see,
A roadmap etched in jest, carefree.

Like walking through stories, with every step,
Where chuckles ripple and silly secrets prep.
A sunflower giggles, with every prep,
As squirrels cartwheel on their nature-set rep.

In embered pathways where joy is the prize,
Twinkling tales bounce beneath the skies.
So join the adventure, let laughter rise,
Through nature's whispers and its bright surprise!

## **Ballet of Colors in the Forest**

In the woods, the hues do dance,
Twisty twirls in a leafy prance.
A squirrel giggles as it observes,
Raccoons in tights, oh how they curve!

Mushrooms wear hats, so fancy and bright,
While breezes laugh, tickling the light.
A blue jay hops, then does a spin,
Nature's stage where silliness begins!

The pine trees sway with a chuckle and sway,
"Join the party!" they merrily say.
Roots tap to the beat of the bouncy brigade,
Even the flowers, in sequins, parade!

A conga line of critters in sync,
Each step a giggle, each glance a wink.
In this leafy theater, wild and grand,
The forest's a circus, all perfectly planned!

## Sunlit Remnants of the Past

Old wooden benches hold stories of cheer,
Where echoes of laughter drift through the years.
A swing set creaks with tales yet untold,
As shadows play tag, so young and so bold!

Sunbeams peek through in a silly game,
Painting the ground like a wacky fame.
A lost shoe chuckles, recalling its run,
While memories bask in the golden fun.

The rusted bike winks with a glimmering grin,
As if to say, 'Oh, let's do it again!'
Time plays its tricks on the heart and the mind,
In the joy of the past, more laughter we find.

Dandelions giggle, all puffy and spry,
With wishes that dance and flutter and fly.
Each gust of wind carries whispers of jest,
In this sunlit arena, we find our best.

## Harmony in the Shades of Change

A rainbow of giggles spills from the trees,
As colors collaborate, trying to please.
The grass gets jealous, turns greener with pride,
While shadows debate who should dance and who hide!

Autumn approaches with a sly little grin,
Whispering secrets through the thick evening din.
"Hey, who needs the sun? I've got flair of my own,
With hues bold and gorgeous, I'll claim my throne!"

Branches high five, trading colors anew,
As squirrels in tuxedos plan a lively debut.
Every gust of wind sends them into a spin,
Even the ground wears a smile on its chin!

Nature's orchestra plays with so much delight,
As everyday moments turn silly and bright.
In this workshop of change, the jokes run amok,
For every color knows how to rock!

## A Collection of Reflective Moments

A puddle mirrors a giggle, quite round,
As clouds drift above without making a sound.
The frog croaks a sonnet, oh what a thrill,
As he lounges on lily pads, totally chill!

Nearby, a snail races, taking his time,
While ants in a conga line look so sublime.
Reflections ripple with chuckles and cheer,
Every ripple a story, whispers to hear!

Underneath the bridge, a turtle just muses,
"Time's just a joke, just check out my excuses!"
While fireflies twinkle, wearing silly hats,
They buzz on by, spilling giggles like brats!

In this place of chuckles, we gather our pride,
Collecting the moments where laughter won't hide.
Every blink of the eye holds a dance and a jest,
In this whimsical world, we all feel our best!

## Nature's Sentinels in Bright Hues

In the breeze, a dance we see,
A riot of colors, oh so free!
A twirl, a tumble, they seem to tease,
As clumsy creatures move with ease.

The squirrel dons a vest so bright,
He struts around in pure delight.
With acorns tucked beneath his chin,
He's ready for a grand game to begin.

A rustling whisper through the trees,
A plot to prank the bumblebees.
They chuckle softly, as they sway,
"Catch us if you can," they say.

In this world of jests and play,
Each color brightens up the day.
So next time you stroll through the park,
Watch for the giggles that sweetly spark.

## A Song of Air and Decomposing Grace

A melody drifts from the ground,
Where hidden treasures can be found.
With worms that wiggle, oh so sly,
They work real hard, but oh, they lie!

The compost crew, a motley bunch,
With critters feasting, munch by munch.
They toss their greens and sneak a snack,
While thinking they're on the right track.

Around the pile, the bugs convene,
In fancy hats, they laugh, they preen.
"Who knew that stinky could be fun?"
Their party rages in the sun.

A serenade from roots below,
As nature's pranksters put on a show.
With laughter echoing all around,
In this chaos, joy is found.

## The Radiance of Change Unveiled


A twist of fate, a swirl of fate,
Old garments shed, they celebrate!
The colors change, but who's to blame?
A party started by the flame!

Mismatched socks in hues so wild,
The trees parade, each one a child.
With branches high, they sway and bow,
Daring the sun to take a vow.

"Shiny objects, our foils so bright,
We'll flash our charms, oh what a sight!"
The sun replies with beams of gold,
While critters giggle, feeling bold.

Across the scene, an artful blur,
As nature winks with a cheeky spur.
In chaos found, a smile is shared,
As life spins round, carefree and dared.

## Under the Spell of Shifting Seasons


When chilly air makes frosty sighs,
And jokester clouds play peekaboo in skies.
The wind, a rascal, rustles past,
With whispers of winter's spell cast.

As snuggly creatures scurry near,
They clutch their snacks and show no fear.
"Oh, look at that!" they shout with glee,
"More snowflakes fall for you and me!"

The seasons play a game of tag,
From sun to snow, a color rag.
With every swirl, another twist,
They laugh aloud, none would resist.

So dance in joy through each phase we see,
A comical romp through life's marquee.
With every turn, a hearty cheer,
Nature's funhouse, forever near.

## Call of the Wild Pastels

Colors smash like jelly beans,
On the ground in vibrant scenes.
Squirrels argue, chasing nuts,
While the sun just giggles, struts.

Fluttering sounds from above,
A panic in the garden glove.
Robin's steal an acorn's fate,
While they dance, it's hard to hate.

Picnic baskets soon will spill,
As ants join in for the thrill.
Nature's pranksters play around,
With jests in every leafy mound.

Winds blow gently, tickle trees,
With whispers carried by the breeze.
Wouldn't trade this cheerful fun,
For shadows from the setting sun.

### Where Brightness Meets the Earth.

A cozy chair with sunlit beams,
Makes chatter blend with daylight dreams.
Grass tickles toes, a playful tease,
As ants march on, like tiny knees.

Kites tangle high above the throng,
Chasing clouds that move along.
Birds drop gossip, with every chirp,
While flowers blush and start to burp.

Jumping puddles, splash and shout,
Who knew fun could be found throughout?
The world is one big giggly place,
With nature owning every space.

As evening falls, the fireflies dance,
Turning dusk into a wiggly trance.
With all this joy, who needs a mirth?
When you find laughter 'neath the earth.

## Whispers of Autumn's Embrace

Crunchy sounds beneath our feet,
A symphony no other can beat.
Pumpkin hats adorned with glee,
Laughing at the squirrel's decree.

Frogs in jackets sing a tune,
While shadows stretch beneath the moon.
In bubbling clouds, the giggles rise,
As feathery friends plot surprise.

Hats go flying, caught in the breeze,
As children shout with squeals, "Oh please!"
With every gust, they tumble down,
Creating chaos, stealing the crown.

Autumn's game, a merry chase,
As nature dons her silly face.
With each twist of fate, there's delight,
In the whispers shared by night.

## **Golden Hues and Soft Shadows**

Sunbeams turn to playful baubles,
Twinkling through the ferny bubbles.
Jokes exchanged by cheeky crows,
As chubby toads strike funny poses.

Painting paths of gold so bright,
Adventurers with grins take flight.
Belly laughs from the garden gnome,
Who gets lost in a whirlwind foam.

Under pies, the critters flit,
Searching for a tasty bit.
Chasing dreams, or maybe dust,
Mischief reigns; in that we trust!

Sundaes dripped from the tree tops,
While honey drips and giggle pops.
To play in hues, both bright and light,
What a hoot! What a silly sight!

## Spectrums of Green in Autumn's Hues

A squirrel in pajamas, what a sight,
Chasing shadows, oh what a fright!
Munching acorns as if they're gold,
Interviewing each leaf, or so I'm told.

A chipmunk joins, in a tiny debate,
On who's the best at snagging a plate.
With twirls and flips, the dance begins,
Nature's stand-up, with furry wins!

A jolly crow caws, with clever jest,
As butterflies try their very best.
To flutter by without falling down,
But they all seem to wear a frown!

The show goes on with giggles and glee,
As branches sway like a scene from TV.
So grab your popcorn, come take a seat,
Nature's comedy, oh so sweet!

# The Artistry of Nature's Palette

A painter on a windy day,
Splattering colors in a silly way.
"Oops! That's not blue!" a branch might say,
Grumbling softly with vines in dismay.

A bunny hops by, checking the hues,
While birds critique their colorful views.
"More pink!" chirps one, adding a twist,
Nature's masterpiece cannot be missed!

A butterfly lands with a flair of sass,
Critiquing each stroke like an art class.
"Not quite right, more spark!" it insists,
As flowers giggle and twirl in bliss.

The artist laughs, and brushes a leaf,
Creating chaos amidst their belief.
Turning the dull into vibrant glee,
In this funny gallery, we all agree!

## Nature's Brushstrokes in Soft Mellow

In a quiet glade, a fox takes a yawn,
Stretched out like a sunbeam at the dawn.
Butterflies juggling, quite the fun show,
While frogs croak along like a froggy flow.

The wind giggles through branches in style,
Tickling the faces, making them smile.
A dance-off begins, with twirls and sways,
Each critter boogieing in their own ways.

An owl sipping tea, gives a wise nod,
Watching the chaos, totally awed.
"Is this art or just nature's lost game?"
As giggles echo, with critters to blame.

With splashes of giggles and colorful scenes,
Nature spins tales in marvelous means.
So let's all chuckle beneath that big tree,
In this mellow madness, just you and me!

## Glowing Trails Through the Canopy

A raccoon in glasses reads a cool book,
While squirrels chime in, "Come take a look!"
With shadows waltzing on a bright stage,
The audience laughs, all lost in the page.

Fireflies winking, like stars on a spree,
Dancing around with glee guaranteed.
"Catch me if you can!" they giggle and glow,
Sprinkling sparkles, quite the funny show.

Word spread fast to the critters nearby,
"Let's throw a party, oh my, oh my!"
The tree trunk quakes with laughter and cheer,
As raccoons start dancing, nothing to fear.

Each bug joins in, with their very own flair,
Turning the night into a bright fair.
So when the moon beams down from above,
We laugh at the silliness, and feel the love!

## Twilight's Hand on Forested Canvas


In the woods where shadows play,
Critters dance in a goofy ballet.
Squirrels argue over acorns too,
While raccoons scheme, plotting their coup.

The sky dips down in orange hues,
As crickets sing their quirky blues.
A bear in a top hat, what a sight!
He tiptoes, hoping to steal some bites.

When the sun winks and starts to yawn,
The pine trees weave a sleepy brawn.
But watch out for the breezy scream,
Grasshoppers hop with a comic dream.

As the night descends on their fun,
Frogs croak tunes of the day undone.
The moon chuckles at the clumsy crew,
In this forest of antics, always anew.

## The Illumination of the Whispering Woods

A glow in the bushes, what could it be?
A raccoon with a light bulb, can't you see?
He stumbles and fumbles, what a show,
As fireflies giggle, saying, "Go, buddy, go!"

With wit in their wings, the moths take flight,
Holding an afterparty deep in the night.
A caterpillar DJ spins a tune,
While worms tap dance under the glowing moon.

The trees are all gossiping, what a chat!
With branches waving like, 'Did you see that?'
A mouse in a tuxedo, feeling so grand,
Serves cheese to the critters, a tasty hand.

So when dusk begins, and colors sway,
Remember this crew in their wild, funny play.
In a world where creatures boogie and glide,
Laughter echoes through the woods, amplified!

## **Chromatic Dreams in Nature's Embrace**

Colors burst forth in a playful spree,
As bunnies in bowties sip herbal tea.
They giggle in gardens, chasing their tails,
While ants wear sombreros, plotting their trails.

The flowers are gossiping, what do they bloom?
One says, "I'm radiant, I'm not just perfume!"
With petals all puffed, they strut with flair,
Like fashion models, flaunting their air.

A hedgehog rolls by in a glorious race,
While daisies cheer, "Come join the chase!"
Buzzing bees flit with a ticklish tease,
As whimsical whispers whip through the leaves.

At dusk, when the world seems to dance and sing,
Frogs suit up in tuxes, pretending to swing.
In this vivid land of eclectic dreams,
Nothing's too silly—we're bursting at the seams!

## Shadows of Color Beneath the Boughs


Under the canopy, where giggles collide,
A turtle wears shades, thinking he's suave.
Goldfish in ponds are the latest fashion,
While clouds form hats, darting with passion.

The squirrels are plotting their comedy bit,
With acorns as props, they never quit!
A rabbit in sneakers hops to the beat,
While butterflies wink, reigniting the heat.

When the sun dips low, it's time to unwind,
With jesters and jokers all intertwined.
Frogs leap like stars, they giggle and croak,
Lost in their humor and delightful poke.

As the moon paints silver on the wild stage,
Creatures combine for a laughable page.
In the shadows of color, don't miss a beat,
Nature's jesters prepare a high-spirited treat!

# The Last Whisper of Celestial Connections

In the garden where giggles stray,
Sunshine spills like melted clay.
Wobbly shadows doing the dance,
Crickets join in, given the chance.

A sunflower wears a smirk so wide,
While daisies gossip and confide.
A snail, the king of slow-paced dreams,
Plans a race with ticklish beams.

The azure sky plays peek-a-boo,
With clouds that puff and drift askew.
Stars chuckle as night takes its turn,
While fireflies laugh in bright lanterns' burn.

All's a jig in this lively glade,
Where shadows and sunshine serenade.
Petals twirl, a frolicsome spree,
Nature's laugh is wild and free.

## Woven Memories of the Earth's Heart

Breezes whisper through the trees,
Carrying tales with the greatest ease.
A squirrel practices acrobats,
While the groundhog cheers in fancy hats.

Jokes sprout from the fertile ground,
Where wobbling mushrooms laugh all around.
A butterfly's wink, a ladybug's grin,
Nature's joke is where all laughs begin.

Picnics of ants with crumbs to share,
Their tiny spread makes all hearts flare.
A worm with style unduly proud,
Does the cha-cha, drawing a crowd.

The earth's pulse taps in rhythmic beats,
As giggles burst from playful feats.
Twirls of joy, bright and absurd,
In this realm, laughter is preferred.

## **Trails of Ember and Echo**

In the twilight where shadows tease,
An owl hoots, swaying with the breeze.
Fireflies plan a disco night,
While crickets strum strings of delight.

Sparks of laughter flutter and prance,
As starlight joins in for the dance.
A fox with a grin, tiptoes along,
To the rhythm of an old folklore song.

The moon beams down, a mischievous grin,
While raccoons sneak snacks, oh where to begin?
The forest floors roll out a rug,
For a gathering, comfy and snug.

Each rustle, a riddle, each twinkle, a jest,
Nature plays games, her very best.
In frolic and glee, worries are tossed,
As shadows delight, no laughter is lost.

## Dancing Shadows in a Whispered Realm

In a glen where jests and giggles bloom,
A rabbit in shades forms a tiny room.
With twigs as microphones, they can sing,
To the beats of a squirrel's chaotically wing.

Pinecone hats and acorn caps,
The woodland's ensemble takes a few naps.
Each branch a stage, each root a seat,
With laughter ringing, oh how sweet!

A breeze tickles branches, trees cavort,
While frogs in tuxedos play a fine sport.
A whimsy parade, a light-hearted jest,
As laughter echoes, they never rest.

The whispers of fun dance through the trees,
Unleashing chuckles with utmost ease.
Here, shadows leap and frolic around,
In this playful haven, joy can be found.

## The Soft Murmur of a Glowing Earth

In the garden, whispers dance,
A celery in pants takes a chance.
Tomatoes giggle, rocking in place,
While carrots try to keep up the pace.

Sunbeams tickle the soil so shy,
A bumblebee sneezes, oh my!
Daisies wear shades, feeling quite grand,
As earthworms plot a conga line band.

Gnomes chuckle as squirrels play tag,
While pumpkins rumble, "Here comes the brag!"
The breeze teases flowers, a playful dart,
Nature's stage, where giggles start.

So come to the party, don't be late,
Where every creature has something great.
With jocular jests and giddy delight,
The soft murmur makes everything right.

## Echoes of the Dying Year

As autumn bids a humorous farewell,
The squirrels hold nuts like a show-and-tell.
Pumpkins sip cocoa, don't be misled,
While the last few flowers put on their bedspread.

Chirps of crickets argue the score,
"Who's winning, the night or the day?" they implore.
Old leaves rattle with stories to spin,
A comic routine from where they've been.

The sun paints shadows, a slapstick array,
As red and gold join in a ballet.
Clouds toss confetti, a visual feast,
Even the breeze joins in, to say the least!

With frosty giggles, it's time to retreat,
But nature winks back, "I won't admit defeat!"
Echoes of laughter weave through the air,
In the dying year, good times we share.

## **Flickering Gold Beneath a Canopy**

Underneath the boughs, it's quite a charade,
Laughter erupts where shadows cascade.
A squirrel in shades and a hat oh-so-fine,
Balances acorns, sipping on brine.

The sunlight winks, a jester it seems,
As mushrooms giggle in their spore-filled dreams.
A rabbit hops by, sporting new jeans,
While butterflies flirt and share funny scenes.

Boughs sway with humor, they chime along,
As breezes hum softly a comical song.
The world is alive, a comedic display,
Down the path where the gigglers play.

In this canopy where laughter unfurls,
Nature has crafted her whimsical pearls.
From the grass to the sky, it's a marvelous sight,
Flickering gold is a stand-up delight.

## A Story Written in Color and Shadow

In the forest's expanse, tales weave and glow,
Frogs tell of dreams while the crickets all know.
A canvas of colors spills forth from the trees,
Caterpillars dance in mid-afternoon breeze.

With splashes of humor, the world plays its part,
While shadows play tag, it's a genuine art.
Raccoons wear wigs; they're dressing with flair,
As starlight twinkles like they just don't care.

Every inch of the ground bursts with laughter anew,
The sky's quizzical blue throws in a clue.
Fireflies perform an electric ballet,
As each color whispers, "Let's party today!"

So gather your chuckles, bring all your friends,
For a story unfolds that never quite ends.
In this vibrant realm where silliness flows,
A tale of delight is where the heart glows.

## Kaleidoscope of the Season's Heart


In a whirl of laughter, colors collide,
Squirrels in capes, oh what a ride!
Jumping through puddles, dancing with cheer,
Chasing their shadows, with giggles to hear.

Sunlight's a jester, casting a spell,
Tickling the petals, oh can't you tell?
With whispers of breeze, they twirl round and round,
Like a playful parade, where joy can be found.

Tiny acorns in hats, so proud and so bold,
Singing old stories, just waiting to be told.
The breeze sways beneath, like a child on a swing,
Making the world feel like a grand, foolish thing.

As daytime wraps up in a blanket of dusk,
Fireflies join in, spreading sparkle and musk.
While critters tell tales that no one can hear,
The season's heart dances, spreading laughter and cheer.

## Reflections on a Gilded Path

Once on a stroll along a grand lane,
A raccoon in boots, what a strange gain!
Waving his paws with a dramatic flair,
Claiming the path was a runway, oh where?

The sun beamed down with a cheeky grin,
As squirrels debated, who'd win the spin.
One twirled too fast, fell into a bush,
As giggles erupted, like a joyful rush.

Leaves in a frenzy, a colorful fight,
With nature's confetti, what a delight!
Each gust of wind brought a chuckle anew,
As the trees laughed too, in their rustling crew.

But the crown jewel was a butterfly's dash,
Wearing a tutu, gone all in a flash!
Onlookers chuckled at the scene so grand,
As shadows stretched long, in a whimsical band.

# A Mosaic of Nature's Secrets

In a garden of giggles, the daisies conspire,
Telling secrets of sunshine, with great desire.
A ladybug in stripes, oh quite the sight,
Dancing with chaos, in sheer delight.

Bumbles buzzed tunes, with their funky beat,
While ants held a concert, with crumbs for a seat.
The sun winks down like a mischievous friend,
As blossoms do prance and the laughter won't end.

Hopscotch with shadows, the game of the day,
Blades of grass giggle, while showing the way.
An owl in a tree, strumming tunes of the night,
With the moon as his crowd, what an odd sight!

The pond's tiny ripples, like diamonds they gleam,
With frogs in a chorus, they hatch a new theme.
Bubbles of joy float, as all nature chimes,
In a mosaic that hums, with laughter that climbs.

## **Glistening Dreams Under the Canopy**

Beneath the great boughs, where the whispers grow,
Sparkling puddles reflect the show.
A snail in a tux, tiptoes by chance,
Craving a spotlight for a slimy dance.

The shy ferns peek from their leafy retreat,
While mushrooms set tables for a quirky meet.
With pies made of moonlight, and tea brewed with glee,
Gather 'round, all ye critters, there's fun for thee!

Twinkling stars giggle, in the morning's gold,
As shadows of critters share laughter untold.
The whispers around, like a playful breeze,
Bringing along stories of squirrels with keys.

But just as the day fades, and the fireflies rise,
We bid adieu to this whimsical prize.
Yet under the canopy, dreams softly gleam,
Where nature serves laughter, our hidden theme.

## The Dance of Dappled Sunlight

In the woods, a game so bright,
Squirrels twirl, a comical sight.
The beams play tag, oh what a tease,
While birds break out in giggles and wheeze.

A shadow slips, then prances away,
While frogs pop up for a quick ballet.
Nature's stage is set, no need to fret,
With every move, a laugh is met.

## When Twilight Meets the Canopy

The moon peeks through, a shy debut,
As critters gather for their night skew.
Crickets chirp their funny tunes,
While raccoons dance under silver moons.

A bat swoops low, it loses its hat,
The owls laugh loud, "Oh, imagine that!"
With each cackle, the night grows bright,
Beneath this stage, it's a silly sight.

## Shifting Colors in the Breeze

Oh, look at that, a color spree,
The vines and blooms, wild and free.
A yellows bob as reds begin to prance,
While blues and greens join in the dance.

Swirling in circles, a prankster's plot,
Yellow's a clown, but purple's quite hot.
With every sway and flip, they tease,
A riot of colors, giggles on the breeze.

## Sun-kissed Petals on the Ground

Oh what a mess, petals everywhere,
A flowery blanket that's hard to bear.
Bumblebees buzz and trip on their feet,
While ants march along and can't take the heat.

Rolling in foam, but look—what a race!
Petals compete for the best landing place.
A floral contest, who will be crowned?
With laughter and chaos, joy is found.

## Caresses in a Sunlit Grove

In the park, I dance with glee,
A tree asks, "What's the fuss with me?"
I say, "I'm just here for some shade,
And catching squirrels in a charade!"

The sunlight tickles my fuzzy hair,
While bees buzz round without a care.
I try to sing a merry tune,
Till a bird joins in, a screeching cartoon!

I trip over roots that come alive,
And giggle as I try to jive.
The grass winks up, so soft, so sweet,
While ants march by on tiny feet!

So here in this sunny, leafy spree,
My heart is light, happy, and free.
With nature's humor all around,
Life's a joke—a joy profound!

## The Quiet Symphony of the Forest Floor

The forest floor hums a quirky tune,
With mushrooms tapping—oh what a boon!
A raccoon's laughter echoes through trees,
While crickets chirp, "Dance if you please!"

A worm wiggles, trying to groove,
As I trip over roots, attempting to move.
Sunbeams giggle, casting warm rays,
Painting shadows in whimsical ways.

A squirrel points out my clumsy twirl,
Then mimics me—oh what a whirl!
The ground tickles feet, an earthy embrace,
Nature's laughter, a playful space!

With every step, I join the jest,
In this cacophony, I feel blessed.
An orchestra of quips and cheer,
In this leafy realm, laughter's clear!

## Radiant Fall: A Journey Within

I wander through a color spree,
Where orange and gold dance with glee.
A leaf flutters down, gives me a wink,
"Catch me if you can!" it dares, I think!

The trees chuckle, wearing their crowns,
As I trip on twigs, falling down.
Pumpkins roll past, their heads held high,
While squirrels laugh and try to fly!

Each step hides giggles beneath my shoe,
Where nature's pranks are ever true.
I chase a gust that plays tag with my hat,
Fruits tumble down like, "Is that where it's at?"

So haphazardly, I dance and twirl,
Among radiant hues, my heart in a whirl.
In this riot of colors, joy's on parade,
In a playful world, adventures are made!

## **Secrets Wrapped in Gossamer Glow**

In twilight's embrace, whispers take flight,
Gossamer secrets drift into night.
A spider grins, spinning tales of delight,
While shadows play hide-and-seek at twilight.

Dewdrops giggle, clinging to leaves,
While bees float past, wearing tiny sleeves.
A glowworm hums its melodic tune,
Dancing in rhythm with the glowing moon.

"Why're you out so late?" the owl hoots clear,
"Chasing mischief?" I nod and cheer.
The world's a circus in radiant bloom,
Each creature laughs in the velvet gloom.

So here I stand, in a giggling show,
With nature's wonders, putting on a glow.
Wrapped in secrets and spots of light,
In this playful realm, everything feels right!

## The Serpent of Time in Spectrum

In hues of green, they pirouette,
As shadows giggle, a dance duet.
With every twist, they mock a rhyme,
Oh, how they tangle, the serpent of time!

Blades of grass wear a leafy crown,
In a swirling game, they tumble down.
A spiral of colors, so silly and bright,
Like squirrels in suits, comical sight!

Whispers of winds play tricks on the ground,
While cheeky critters jump all around.
Is that a bug with a tiny mustache?
Or a feathered friend in a flamboyant flash?

A rainbow's tail flips, a giggle it brings,
As it tickles the sun on its shiny wings.
Caught in the moment, we say with delight,
What a grand show, oh, what a silly sight!

## The Glimmering Adieu of Summer

The sun wears shades, feeling quite cool,
As summer's bow takes a plunge in the pool.
A final goodbye, with zesty confetti,
While crickets play tunes, oh so sweaty!

Pine cones giggle, tucked in the breeze,
As squirrels throw acorns like some funny tease.
With umbrellas up in a game of charades,
Who knew summer had such silly parades?

The colors all dance, just like old fools,
While bees don tiny sunglasses as rules.
What's that in the air? Is it humor mixed sweet?
A taste of the sun baked in nature's retreat?

As twilight descends, stars twinkle and wink,
In a fit of laughter, no time left to think.
With giggles and grins, we raise up a cheer,
For summer's farewell, it's that time of year!

# Threads of Nostalgia in Every Shade

In patches of color, memories swirl,
Like old school photos of that goofy girl.
A tangle of laughter, wrapped up in gold,
With stories so funny, they never grow old!

Each hue tells a tale with a wink and a grin,
Of moments forgotten, where silliness begins.
With every flutter, a chuckle escapes,
As the yarns of the past weave quirky landscapes.

A patchwork of visions, stitched with a joke,
Where every thread ties a smile to evoke.
From bronzed autumns to vibrant spring,
A tapestry of laughter's the joy that we bring!

So gather around for a laugh and a cheer,
As nostalgia dances, bringing us near.
With every shade that colors our day,
We find humor lurking, in every old play!

## Harbinger of Time on Nature's Canvas

On a canvas of giggles, hues blend and spin,
While creatures conspire to plot and grin.
What's this? A brush with a painter's delight,
Or a prankster who juggles, both furry and bright!

The tick-tock of laughter, a chorus in play,
As moments and memories frolic away.
With dappled reflections, the sunset does tease,
Like jolly old jesters caught on the breeze.

Whirling in circles, a merry dance crew,
Of butterflies dreaming in shades of blue.
As the sun dips below with a theatrical flair,
We chuckle at shadows that frolic in air!

Each brushstroke of joy paints the world with a wink,
As nature's own mirth leaves us smiling, I think.
So here's to the giggles, the fun, and the cheer,
For life's art is funny, year after year!

## When Colors Beneath Whisper

When the sun tries to tickle a tree,
The branches giggle, oh so carefree.
A dance of hues, a color parade,
Nature's jesters, never afraid.

Squirrels chuckle, with acorn hats,
Chasing shadows and playful spats.
A breeze brings laughter, in giggly swirls,
As nature plays pranks on the world.

The ground is a canvas, oh what a sight,
A jigsaw of giggles from morning to night.
Dandelions are crowns on heads so small,
In this green kingdom, we're all having a ball.

When twilight's blush starts to tease,
All creatures wear smiles, a playful breeze.
So come join the fun, take a quick peek,
At the whimsical world where colors speak!

## The Brush of Evening's Glow


As the sun dips low with a wink and a grin,
The sky splashes orange, and the day wears a fin.
Clouds become artists with wild strokes and flair,
Painting the horizon, unaware of their hair.

Critters are prancing in twilight's embrace,
Chasing around with a hop and a trace.
A firefly flickers, a tiny flash dance,
In this brilliant gallery, don't miss your chance!

The crickets recite their quirky old tunes,
As shadows grow longer beneath the balloons.
A game of hide and seek, who's it to be?
As mischief is brewing near the old oak tree.

So laugh with the night, wear your sparkling smile,
For every odd twinkle is worth your while.
In the brush of the dusk, let your spirit unfold,
In a world filled with giggles and tales to be told!

## Radiant Trails of Whispering Shades

A parade of butterflies in silly formation,
Crashing into petals, what a sensation!
Yellow surprises, the pinks are a tease,
Even the daisies engage in the spree.

Oh look at the shadows, forming a gang,
All the giggles from nature, oh what a clang!
They tumble and roll, not a care in sight,
In the funny, vibrant embrace of the night.

A chase through the meadows, away from the fuss,
The playful gazelles join in without a fuss.
The bushes are chuckling, their secrets they hold,
With stories of silliness, daring and bold.

So revel in colors, with a wink and a jig,
Nature's a jokester, come dance a small gig.
In this radiant chaos, let humor flow free,
In every shade fluttering, there's always a spree!

## Mellow Echoes in Nature's Vault

In the mellow shadows where giggles reside,
The trees tell tales of sticky green pride.
A parrot squawks jokes in a feathery throng,
While crabs in the pond sing their silly song.

Ripples of mischief race over the lake,
It's not just the fish that love to partake.
With frogs in tuxedos, hopping with grace,
They leap into antics, maintaining the pace.

As the stars come out, they twinkle and play,
Mirrors of laughter from the end of the day.
Grains of sand whisper secrets of old,
In the echoes, a tapestry of humor unfolds.

So gather around with a twinkle in your eye,
Embrace all the chuckles that quietly sigh.
In nature's own vault, let the laughter bloom,
With hilarious tales in every room!

# The Caress of the Golden Hour

Sunshine winks through branches wide,
Little shadows take a ride.
Squirrels laugh as they scamper around,
Chasing beams that dance on the ground.

A chatty bird plays peekaboo,
With the glint of dusk as its view.
Caught in laughter, the world seems bright,
In this funny, warm, glowing light.

In a game of tag, the colors blend,
Where the day mingles with night, my friend.
The trees wear hues like jackets bright,
While shadows cringe, but can't lose sight.

So come, let's giggle at the scene,
Where day and night are silly and keen.
With each tick-tock, the fun does grow,
In this golden hour, just watch it flow.

## Sylvan Dances of Color and Shade

Whirl like a leaf in a breezy swirl,
Watch the colors as they twirl.
The sun's a prankster, a trickster bold,
Spilling warmth from its pot of gold.

Grass tickles toes in a playful tease,
While branches wave as if to say, "Please,
Join us in this dance so grand,
Where giggling shadows take a stand!"

The flowers join in with a lively jig,
Bouncing about, dancing big.
A butterfly flutters like it's on cue,
Cracking jokes only nature knew.

And as we twirl in this merry spree,
Wondering what else we might foresee,
Let's laugh at how the world seems to sway,
In this hilarious forest ballet!

## Hush of Breeze in a Painted Wilderness

A gentle whisper makes trees giggle,
While flowers sway and do a wiggle.
The breeze hears jokes from unseen lips,
Carrying chuckles with every trip.

Cartwheeling clouds in a sky so blue,
Play hide and seek, just me and you.
The air is thick with silly fun,
As crickets join with their evening drum.

The owls hoot with a wink and a nod,
Even the mushrooms look good and odd.
A rustling laugh from the ground below,
Emerging critters putting on a show.

So hush, you'll hear the wilderness clown,
In this vibrant space of colorful brown.
With giggles tucked among the stars,
Nature's a comedian—don't forget who you are!

## The Glow of Time's Gentle Ruin

As day drips into twilight's grace,
The sun trips over its own bright face.
Trees chuckle softly, sharing a jest,
While shadows stretch, putting humor to test.

Old rocks grumble about their age,
Trying to keep up with the stage.
A laugh from the brook settles like cream,
As time plays tricks, like a whimsical dream.

Colors blush, not ready to fade,
Throwing a party in nature's glade.
And as the stars begin to peep,
The world grows drowsy, ready for sleep.

Yet in the glow of what used to be,
Giggling echoes still roam free.
So let's toast to time, its soft caress,
In this funny chaos, we find our mess!

## The Dance of Branches and Beams

In the breeze, they swirl and twirl,
Like dancers in a merry whirl.
Tiptoeing over trunk and limb,
They chuckle loud, a cheerful hymn.

A squirrel joins in with a leap,
While rabbits laugh, their antics steep.
The shadows giggle as they play,
In nature's jest, they spend the day.

The sun peeks in, with a wink so sly,
Casting tricks as it passes by.
A wink here and a flick there,
Results in giggles everywhere!

As day gives way to evening's glow,
The branches sway and steal the show.
In this hilarious, vibrant scene,
The forest feels like a foxtrot dream!

## Verdant Visions Under Radiant Skies

With hues so bright, they play their part,
As if the stars fell from the heart.
The grass tickles to make you giggle,
In warm embrace, leaves twist and wiggle.

The clouds above dance like they're fairs,
While shadows blend in foolish pairs.
A butterfly chases its tale,
While critters laugh without a fail.

Oh, sun beams down with cheeky grins,
And every bug gets in on sins.
They skip and slide on paths so green,
In this wild jest, nothing's routine!

Every rustle brings a new surprise,
A symphony of goofy cries.
As laughter echoes, pure delight,
A canvas painted in sheer light.

## Flickers of Life in the Forest's Heart

In a cozy nook where chuckles grow,
Life flits about, all in a row.
A chipmunk's charm, the rabbit's cheer,
Bring smiles to all who wander near.

Each flicker shows a silly game,
Where shadows romp, no two the same.
A butterfly slips on its own wing,
And every creature starts to sing.

Sunbeams tickle with a gentle touch,
While buzzing bees don't know too much.
They sway and sway, lose track of time,
In this merry rhyme, life feels sublime!

As winks of dusk draw laughter tight,
Every twinkle leads to a fright.
The forest's heart keeps beating strong,
In a funny dance, where all belong!

## Echoes of Color Beneath the Sky

Once upon a flicker of red,
A bird chuckled, 'You heard what I said?'
A joke flitted on the nose of a fox,
Who snorted loud, then put on socks!

The blue above, like giggles spilled,
Echoed tales that funny critters filled.
A raccoon wearing shades, a tiny hat,
Declared himself the best at 'chit-chat!'

Each pulse of hue, a comical thrill,
As squirrels audition for the best 'still.'
They pose like models in the trees,
While ants march past with such unease.

At twilight's end, the hues collide,
In this jest of nature, wild and wide.
With chuckles echoing, all seems right,
In colorful chaos, a joyful sight!

## Symphony of Fern and Flame

In the forest, a band of greens,
With giggles and wiggles, they dance on scenes.
A trumpet of crickets, a beat from the bees,
Making music with rustles, what a joy to seize!

Bouncing branches play peek-a-boo,
Tickling toes of the squirrels too.
An acorn rolls by, like a bowling ball,
While shadows crack jokes, laughing with all!

The sun winks down through the playful boughs,
While cheeky little flowers take their bows.
A conga line forms, oh what a sight,
In this curious carnival, everything's right!

Nature's a stage, a comedic delight,
Where sass and humor take off in flight.
So join in the fun, let your spirit take aim,
In this vibrant arena, we're all in the game!

## Gentle Glimmers Through the Foliage

A glimmer of fun caught my eye,
As dandelions giggled and danced up high.
The sunbeams tickled a caterpillar near,
Who spun in a circle, filled with cheer!

A light-hearted breeze joins the playful show,
As shadows chase sun spots down below.
The daisies joke about their silly hats,
While trees share tales of their acorn chats!

Fickle rays jump from branch to branch,
While mushrooms do a wiggly little dance.
With each gentle rustle, the laughter is found,
In this funny world where joy abounds!

So how about a game of hide and seek?
With twinkling spots giving us a peek!
Let's prance like the critters, let the good times roll,
In this brighthearted realm, we're on a stroll!

# Echoes of Warmth in the Woods

A sunbeam slips on a banana peel,
And down it goes, how surreal!
Laughter echoes from the rocks and trees,
As shadows shake their floppy knees!

The bushes chatter with a giddy air,
Telling stories, stripping off their care.
Each whisper wraps up in a twinkling cheer,
What a wild ruckus, it's kin to a beer!

A pesky squirrel throws down a nut,
It bounces and tumbles, oh what a cut!
While a sunbeam giggles at the playful jest,
Outdoor antics surely are the best!

With each twinkle and turn, we spin with delight,
In this merry realm, let's dance till night!
So come on, dear friend, let's not resist,
In this jolly kingdom, we shall coexist!

## **Glade of Sunbeams and Shifting Hues**

A giggle from greens as colors collide,
Shades of funfulness spread far and wide.
Sunrays play tag with a breeze full of glee,
While doodle bugs hum their legacy!

Rainbow whispers flutter with such flair,
On branches that twirl like they haven't a care.
The shadows try to catch the sparkling light,
But end up doing the can-can, what a sight!

Hues splatter laughter on flowers so bright,
Each one a story, each one a slight.
As petals poke fun at the clouds drifting by,
In this charming arena, we all start to fly!

So let's twirl through the glade together and laugh,
Join in the fun, let's take a warm bath.
In this silly garden where jokes freely bloom,
We'll dance to the rhythm, dispelling all gloom!

## Beauty in the Year's Farewell

The trees wear coats of orange and gold,
While squirrels act all crazy and bold.
They gather their acorns with frantic glee,
Planning for winter and sippin' their tea.

A breeze gives a shiver, a tickle, a laugh,
While pumpkins grin wide on the garden path.
The scarecrow winks as he guards the corn,
He's probably just jealous of how we're adorned!

With shadows that dance in a playful spin,
I trip on a root, then back up again.
Nature's farewell, a hilarious show,
With signs that suggest it's time to go slow!

So here's to the quirks as the seasons all fade,
And laughter is sprinkled, like colorful shade.
We gather the memories, store them with cheer,
To chuckle and share when the next spring draws near.

# A Sun-dappled Journey Through Nature's Heart

Strolling beneath a patchwork dome,
Where wild critters seem to call it home.
A butterfly flirts with my nose on the trail,
It tickles and dances; oh, I mustn't fail!

The chatter of birds, a quirky affair,
Their jokes flying high, the world's in their care.
I try to join in, but all they do is stare,
With feathers ruffling in the warm, sunny air.

Mushrooms pop up like odd little hats,
I wonder who wore them and why they went splat?
They giggle as raindrops start to fall down,
Nature's own circus, no time for a frown!

As I dance with the shadows and skip with the light,
I trip on a root as I take flight.
With laughter and love in this quirky old glade,
I find warmth in the smiles that the critters have made.

## **Enchanted Tints in Nature's Embrace**

Colors are splashing, a whimsical sight,
While bees wear top hats, oh what a delight!
The flowers are giggling, just bursting with cheer,
As the petals all dance, they know spring is near.

A frog in a tux tries to croak a good song,
While dragonflies spin like they're living all wrong.
I burst out in laughter as they twirl all around,
It's a cabaret party without a dull sound!

The stream trips along like it's late for a date,
With rocks wearing moss, they just can't be late!
The whispers of breezes float in with a grin,
As I join in the revelry and let the fun begin!

In this dazzle of color, I find joy and play,
With nature's own laughter guiding my way.
Each shade tells a story, a harmonious rhyme,
As I twirl with the magic, forgetting all time.

## A Tapestry of Nature's Remnants

In the corner of this patchy green world,
Old treasures lie hidden, with stories unfurled.
A log's a great pirate, oh what tales it will share,
While snails plot a heist without a single care.

The wind plays a tune with a rustle and sigh,
It tailors the echoes, a soft lullaby.
Forgotten old hats made of twigs and of fluff,
Are perfect for rabbits; oh, that's just enough!

A puddle reflects all the chaos around,
A mirror of mischief, with giggles unbound.
The grass shakes its head, whispering loud,
"Let's dance with the clouds; I feel oh so proud!"

So here in this canvas, full of quirks and fun,
Nature creates laughter for everyone.
With remnants and treasures, we'll play all day long,
For in this wild wonder, we all belong!

## Portrait of Silence and Splendor

In the green where whispers dwell,
A squirrel plays the jester's role.
Hiding acorns, ringing bells,
While fungus tosses in his bowl.

A toad croaks tunes of gentle grace,
His friends all laugh, no need for shame.
A ladybug joins the wild chase,
Dancing round, they play the game.

Beneath the shade of leafy crowns,
The sunlight tickles every mood.
Nature's court, no king or crowns,
Just merry critters in a brood.

They throw a party with no plans,
Where vines swing high and mushrooms sway.
As time forgets to make demands,
Life's a jest on a sunny day.

## An Interlude in a Sylvan Ballet

Underneath the bustling boughs,
Frogs don top hats, in the fray.
Crickets bow, and woodpeckers browse,
As bugs form lines for their ballet.

Sunbeams waltz through every groove,
The forest floor's a stage today.
With every jump and every move,
Even ants can't help but sway.

A rabbit hops, a star is born,
While chipmunks hum a catchy tune.
Around their feet, the wildflowers adorn,
A jolly show, a sunlit boon.

The curtain falls, the sun inclines,
As dancers take their final bow.
In this grand tale of nature's signs,
All join in laughter—come, take a vow!

## A Serenade Under Shaded Canopies

The branches sway, a banjo strums,
While foxes stomp their paws in cheer.
A raccoon chimes with merry drums,
    In this theater, fun is near.

With shadows casting stories grand,
    A hedgehog croons a silly tune.
Beneath the stars, they take a stand,
And twirl around the glowing moon.

Squirrels form a vocal band,
With nuts and berries as their shows.
Their beats, my friend, are quite unplanned,
    They sing of acorns and of woes.

No one sits still; a lively spree,
With giggles echoing through the trees.
In this sweet spot, wild and free,
    Nature sighs in joyful glees.

## Timeless Moments in Nature's Glow

With every rustle, laughter swells,
A hedgehog juggles with delight.
The sunshine slips down secret wells,
As shadows stretch to greet the night.

In the dance of rays and silly pranks,
A turtle slips and does a spin.
The giggles bounce along the banks,
As time forgets where it begins.

Fireflies glow, a disco scene,
While butterflies flutter to the beat.
They twist and twirl, both light and keen,
Unruly dancers on their feet.

In moments sweet, the world does play,
And every creature shares a smile.
With nature's charm, they sway away,
Reminding us—it's worth our while.

## A Mosaic of Flora and Glimmer

In the park where odd folks tread,
Giggling flowers play a game,
With sunbeams racing overhead,
And petals whispering my name.

A daisy tried to hop and skip,
While tulips danced in jester's shoes,
A caterpillar made a trip,
To join the fun, he couldn't lose.

Though grasshoppers croaked a tune,
And bees buzzed like they're on a spree,
The breeze swept in, a wobbly rune,
And tickled all the stems with glee.

So here's to blooms in whimsy's reign,
Who tickle hearts with green delight,
A day of joy with no refrain,
In nature's show of giggles bright.

## The Flicker of Day in the Green World

When morning sneezes golden rays,
The critters jive in leafy bars,
A squirrel sneaks in comical ways,
While sunbeams twirl like furry cars.

Awkward dances from the nooks,
Where bunnies hop on everyday,
And wise old owls read funny books,
Squinting at the antics on display.

The shadows laugh beneath the trees,
They noodle 'round, it seems so clear,
A giggling gust floats through the leaves,
And every creature joins the cheer.

So come and frolic, take a seat,
At nature's quirky, merry fest,
With every rustle, every beat,
The world is odd, but never less.

## Tints and Tones in Nature's Symphony

A canvas sprawls with brushy strokes,
The bluebirds prance in silly skirts,
While ants might tell the funniest jokes,
   As butterflies in waltz convert.

A shadow passed, a giggling breeze,
With squirrels working on a heist,
Plucking nuts like they own the trees,
The sun grinned wide, quite enticed.

In every hue, a chuckle brews,
The croaking frogs like chorus kings,
With all these colors, none to lose,
Who could resist the joy it brings?

So sip the laughter in the air,
Let nature woo you with its song,
In every hue, a joyful flare,
An orchestra where all belong.

## Glimmers of Spirit in the Shady Hearth

Under arches where shadows play,
The critters host a hilarious bash,
In corners where they hide and sway,
With silly antics, all in a flash.

A rabbit hops with a top hat flair,
While geese debate on who can quack,
The scene unfolds in laughter's air,
With nature's charm, there's no lack.

The flowers bloom in goofy grins,
As rays of warmth just ripple through,
With buzzing friends in happy spins,
Each moment felt, a comedy cue.

So here we dwell, in joy's embrace,
With chuckles from the boughs above,
In this wacky, playful place,
Each shadow bright with laughter's love.

## **Vivid Mosaics of Earth's Palette**

Colors dance in a whimsical sway,
While critters pretend to have their say.
Beneath the branches, squirrels conspire,
Stealing snacks from the woodland choir.

Ants march on with a comedic stride,
Plotting a picnic, though they can't hide.
Grass blades peek through, their laughter bright,
Joining the fun in their own delight.

A rabbit hops, with a flip and a dash,
Unaware of the snack it may splash.
With every bounce comes a giggling crew,
"Who knew the great outdoors was a zoo?"

As sunlight filters, they start to prance,
Each shadow casting a silly dance.
Nature chuckles in hues so spry,
Creating a scene that makes the heart fly.

## Shadows Weaving tales Beneath

Under the cover of a funny tree,
Goblins and gnomes sip tea with glee.
They whisper tales of their silly ways,
Riding on mushrooms for endless days.

The wind shares secrets in a playful tone,
While pickles and pies roll across the stone.
Caterpillars giggle at the bugs' parade,
In this laughter fest, no pranks are delayed.

A snail in a hat spins circles and grins,
Delighted by leaf-boys and their twin fins.
The shadows stretch, laughter fills the air,
As creatures assemble in a frolicsome square.

To watch this circus, one must be sly,
For this joyous show will make you cry.
With every jest, the forest combines,
To weave a tapestry of funny designs.

## Soft Rays Beneath the Canopy

Bright rays tickle the ground like a cat,
While critters giggle, tipping their hat.
A frog leaps up, not noticing a shoe,
Bouncing back quick, as though it just flew!

A fox tells tales with a wink in its eye,
Of acorns that dance and butterflies shy.
Squirrels take stage on their branches so wide,
Practicing tricks for their nutty slide.

Mushrooms burst out, all dressed in their best,
With polka-dot caps, they join in the quest.
As shadows tumble, they spin with flair,
Creating a stage where all creatures dare.

With laughter echoing through every leaf,
The forest is full of joy, not grief.
Nature's own comedy unfolds in a scene,
Where sunlight and mischief paint all that's green.

## The Sun's Canvas of Soft Decay

As autumn creeps in, the colors clash,
Creating a quilt of a gentle splash.
Bugs wear their coats, all itchy and warm,
While trees tell stories of losing their charm.

The ground is a smorgasbord, crunchy and crisp,
Crickets serenade with their evening lisp.
An old crow salutes with a wink and a squawk,
Holding court on a fence, it starts to mock.

The twilight dances with a bubbly glee,
While shadows stretch out, wild as can be.
Two acorns debate on who's got the style,
"Your cap's all lopsided, but mine's got a mile!"

In this artwork of giggles, both funny and bright,
Where the world grows soft, that's where we delight.
Nature's palette changes, with every turn,
In a charming spectacle, we live and learn.

www.ingramcontent.com/pod-product-compliance
Lightning Source LLC
Chambersburg PA
CBHW070314120526
44590CB00017B/2672